Amazing Animals

Wild Whales

Addition and Subtraction

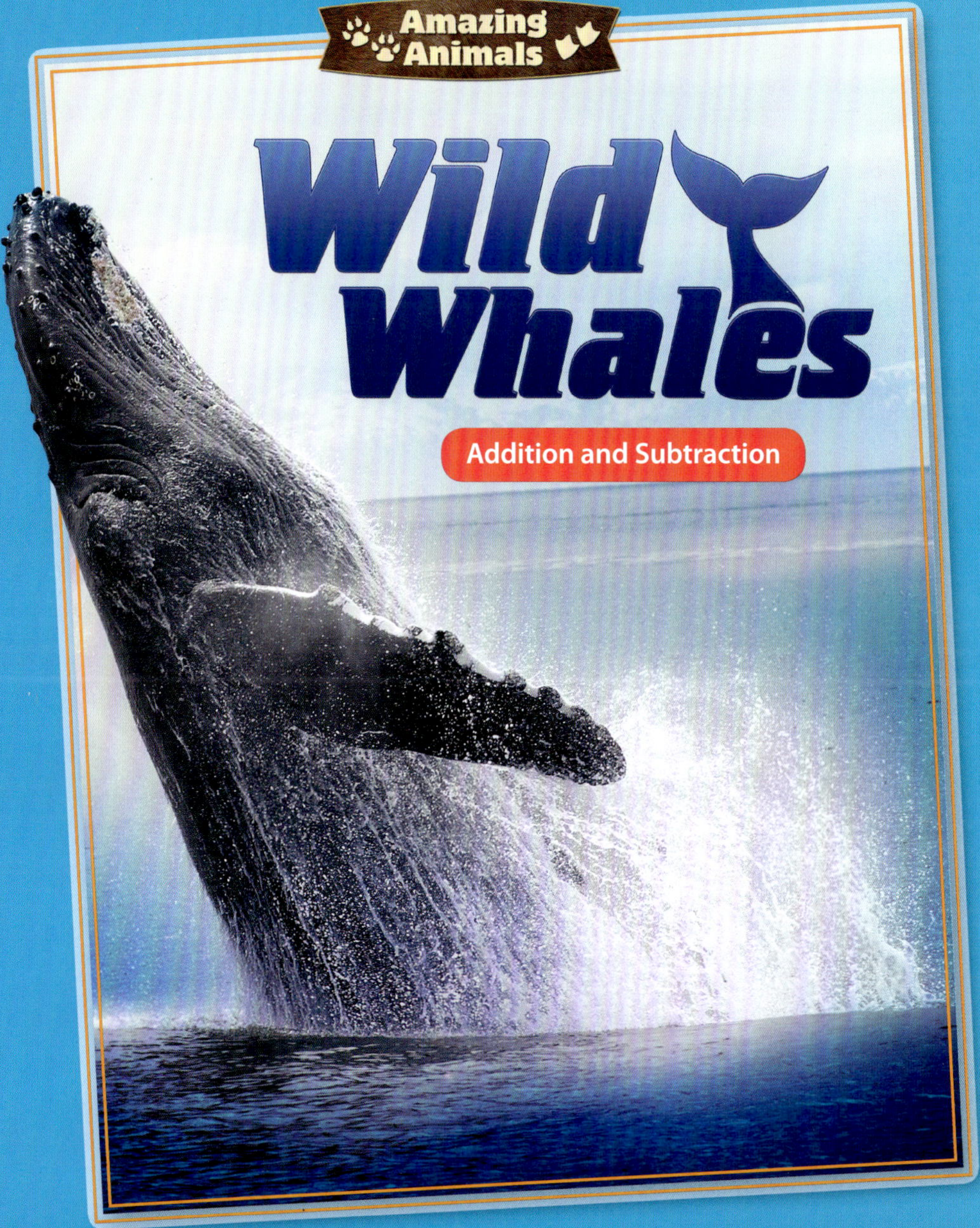

Melissa Pioch, M.Ed.

Consultants

Michele Ogden, Ed.D
Principal, Irvine Unified School District

Jennifer Robertson, M.A.Ed.
Teacher, Huntington Beach City School District

Publishing Credits

Rachelle Cracchiolo, M.S.Ed., *Publisher*
Conni Medina, M.A.Ed., *Managing Editor*
Dona Herweck Rice, *Series Developer*
Emily R. Smith, M.A.Ed., *Series Developer*
Diana Kenney, M.A.Ed., NBCT, *Content Director*
Stacy Monsman, M.A., *Editor*
Kevin Panter, *Graphic Designer*

Image Credits: p. 8 Paul Nicklen/Getty Images; p. 9 (top left) Sylvain Cordier/Getty Images, (bottom) wwing/Getty Images; p. 12 Paul Nicklen/Getty Images; pp. 12-13 Michelle Valberg/Getty Images; p. 14 Scott Olson/Getty Images; p. 15 Hiroya Minakuchi/Getty Images; p. 16 Kenneth Canning/Getty Images; p. 17 Francois Gohier/VWPics/Alamy Stock Photo; p. 19 robertharding/Alamy Stock Photo; p. 22 Tui De Roy/Getty Images; p. 23 PF-(usna1)/Alamy Stock Photo; p. 24 (top) Sciepro/Science Photo Library, (bottom) Ingo Wagner/dpa/picture-alliance/Newscom; p. 25 Flip Nicklin/Getty Images; p. 27 FangXiaNuo/Getty Images; all other images from iStock and/or Shutterstock.

Library of Congress Cataloging-in-Publication Data

Names: Pioch, Melissa, author.
Title: Wild whales / Melissa Pioch, M.Ed.
Description: Huntington Beach, CA : Teacher Created Materials, [2017] | Series: Amazing animals | Audience: K to grade 3. | Includes index. | Description based on print version record and CIP data provided by publisher; resource not viewed.
Identifiers: LCCN 2016053304 (print) | LCCN 2017012088 (ebook) | ISBN 9781480758599 (eBook) | ISBN 9781480757950 (pbk.)
Subjects: LCSH: Whales--Juvenile literature. | Addition--Juvenile literature. | Subtraction--Juvenile literature.
Classification: LCC QL737.C4 (ebook) | LCC QL737.C4 P567 2017 (print) | DDC 599.5--dc23
LC record available at https://lccn.loc.gov/2016053304

Teacher Created Materials

5301 Oceanus Drive
Huntington Beach, CA 92649-1030
http://www.tcmpub.com

ISBN 978-1-4807-5795-0

© 2018 Teacher Created Materials, Inc.
Printed in China WAI002

Table of Contents

Don't Call Them Fish! 4

Toothed Whales 6

Baleen Whales 16

Protecting Whales 26

Problem Solving 28

Glossary 30

Index 31

Answer Key 32

Don't Call Them Fish!

Where does an orca go for braces? The orca-dontist! Why was the whale so sad? Because he was a blue whale!

All jokes aside, whales are interesting animals. There are over 80 **species** of whales, including the orca and blue whale that took starring roles in those jokes! Whales in the wild live their entire lives in ocean waters. But, they are not fish.

Whales are **mammals**, like cats, dogs, and humans. Whales have lungs and need to breathe air. They cannot breathe underwater, so they have to swim to the surface to breathe. Whales breathe through **blowholes** on the tops of their heads. They take in air through the blowhole when they reach the water's surface.

Like all mammals, whales give birth to their babies and feed them milk. Whale babies are called calves. Calves aren't small like other animals' infants. In fact, when baby blue whales are born, they are already the same size as adult elephants!

a gray whale's blowholes

humpback whale and calf

Toothed Whales

What sets toothed whales apart from other whales? You guessed it—teeth! There are about 65 species of toothed whales. Toothed whales are hunters. They chase and eat fish, starfish, crabs, squid, and other ocean animals. Their sharp teeth grip **prey** to prevent escape. Once they have the prey in their grasp, they can swallow it whole or in chunks.

Most toothed whales find their prey with the help of **echolocation**. It helps them "see" in the ocean's dark waters. So, how does it work? Well, toothed whales emit sounds from their foreheads. Those sounds bounce off objects and return to the whales (the sounds echo). The quicker sounds bounce back, the closer objects are. Whales use this information to find nearby food.

Sound Waves Sent by the Whale   Returning Sound Waves

Orcas are the most widely known toothed whale.

Belugas are toothed whales known for their white coloring.

Orcas force a school of fish into a tight ball.

Orcas

What has a black body, a white belly, and can jump through the air? (No, this is not a joke.) It's an orca. Orcas, or killer whales, are ocean **predators** that can eat up to 500 pounds (225 kilograms) of food each day.

Orcas live and hunt together in **pods**. They hunt seals, penguins, sharks, and even other whales. Orcas catch their prey in many ways. Sometimes, they swim around a group of fish. The movement forces the fish into a tight ball. Then, the orcas slap the fish with their tails. This stuns the fish. Orcas also make waves by moving their fins and tails. Seals and penguins on nearby blocks of ice lose their balance in the unsteady water.

Once orcas catch their prey, they do not chew. Instead, they swallow most of their meals whole. Sea lions and small seals slide down easily. Sharks and whales are swallowed as chunks.

An orca breaches close to shore.

An orca quickly approaches seals in shallow water.

LET'S EXPLORE MATH

Orcas have about 45 teeth that are shaped to tear and rip apart prey.

1. How many teeth would two orcas have?
2. How many teeth would four orcas have?
3. How can the solution to the first problem help you solve the second problem?

model of orca teeth

Sperm Whales

Unlike other whales, sperm whales are easy to identify because of their huge, round heads. They are the largest of the toothed whales. They also have the largest brain of any animal that has ever been found on Earth.

Sperm whales' heads hold a lot of fluid. Scientists think that the fluid helps the whales dive deep. They have found that the fluid turns into wax when it is cold. Since the wax is **denser** than the fluid, it weighs the whale down. As the sperm whale swims closer to the surface, the water gets warmer. This causes the wax to melt again. Sperm whales use this ability to hunt in both deep and shallow waters. They can dive over 3,000 feet (900 meters) to look for prey.

LET'S EXPLORE MATH

Imagine that a sperm whale wants to dive 3,160 feet to catch a squid. It dives 520 feet. Then, it dives another 1,490 feet.

How much farther does the sperm whale have to dive to reach a depth of 3,160 feet?

giant squid

Narwhals

Narwhals are sometimes called the Unicorns of the Sea. They are toothed whales best known for their long tusks. The tusk is really a tooth that grows from the male's upper jaw. Females can grow this tusk, too, but it is much less common. And when they do, the tusk is not as long as a male's. Male tusks can grow up to 9 ft. (3 m) long and can weigh more than 22 lbs. (10 kg).

A narwhal surfaces to breathe.

A pod of narwhals passes through Arctic Bay in Canada.

Scientists are still studying why narwhals have tusks. Some scientists think they use the tusks to fight other males or to impress females. But, the tusks have lots of nerves and tiny holes that let water in. So, narwhals may use their tusks to tell how warm and salty the water is. This might help them find prey. Or, it might help them find their way in the ocean.

LET'S EXPLORE MATH

1. A pod of narwhals is swimming together. A group of 14 swim away to find food. Now, there are 78 narwhals. How many narwhals were originally in the pod?

2. A different pod of narwhals is swimming together. Then, 15 more join them. Now, there are 60 narwhals. How many narwhals were in the pod before the new narwhals arrived?

Beluga Whales

Beluga whales are related to narwhals and are often a favorite of whale lovers. Their white color and round heads set them apart from other whales, as does their playful nature. The beluga is one of the smallest species of whale. Even so, they can reach up to 20 ft. (6 m) long! Calves are born gray or brown, but fade to white when they are about five years old.

Belugas live in cold Arctic waters. They have thick layers of fat, or **blubber**. The blubber helps them stay warm in the cold water. Belugas live in pods and are social whales. They like to "talk" to each other. They talk by clicking and whistling. Belugas can copy other sounds, too.

Belugas also have very flexible necks. They can turn their heads up, down, and side to side. Belugas can even swim backward!

A three-month old beluga calf swims with his mother at the John G. Shedd Aquarium in Chicago, Illinois.

Three playful beluga whales blow bubbles.

Baleen Whales

Baleen whales are different from toothed whales. First, they have two blowholes instead of one. Second, they do not have teeth. Instead, baleen whales have bristles called **baleen plates**. These plates are made of the same protein as our fingernails and hair.

Baleen plates look just like combs. And they act like them too! First, a whale opens its mouth and sucks in prey and water. Then, the water is pushed back through the baleen plates. The plates strain food, which is trapped in the whale's mouth until it is swallowed whole. Each mouthful can hold a million or more tiny animals.

Since baleen whales do not have teeth, they usually eat large amounts of very small animals. The animals include plankton, cyclops, and krill. Krill are a lot like tiny shrimp. A huge whale might eat thousands of pounds of prey in one day.

a gray whale's baleen plates

These time-lapse images of a humpback whale breaching show it jumping out of the water, turning, and falling backward.

Gray Whales

When people see gray whales for the first time, they are often surprised. Gray whales look like they are covered in white spots. The spots are actually **barnacles**. These small creatures attach to gray whales and catch a ride for the rest of their lives. In that time, they eat plankton. In exchange, the barnacles act like **armor** for the whale. Since gray whales grow to about 45 ft. (14 m) long, many barnacles can find a place to attach—up to 1,000 of them!

Gray whales make one of the longest **migrations** of any mammal. They travel more than 10,000 miles (16,000 kilometers) each year. They spend the summer feeding in cool Arctic waters. When the weather gets too cold, they swim south along the Pacific coast. By winter, they reach the warm waters of Mexico. They give birth to their calves there. When spring arrives, the gray whales head north again. In their lifetime, gray whales travel distances that equal a trip to the moon and back!

Barnacles cover a gray whale.

gray whales

LET'S EXPLORE MATH

A gray whale swam 18 miles on Monday. It swam 26 miles Tuesday. By Wednesday, it had traveled a total of 72 miles.

1. How many total miles did the gray whale swim on Monday and Tuesday?

2. How many miles did the gray whale swim on Wednesday?

gray whale migration route

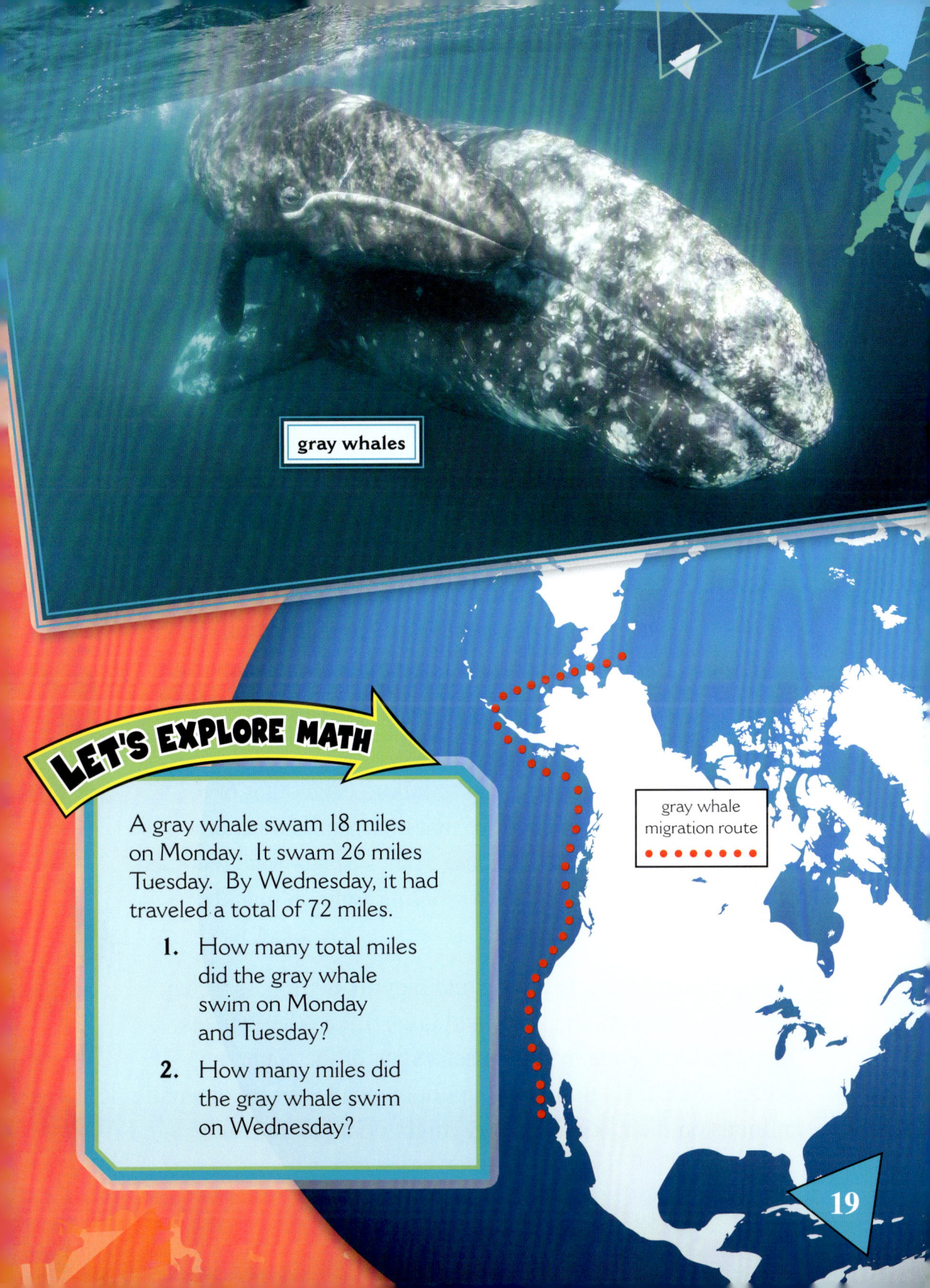

19

a breaching humpback

Humpback Whales

Another species of baleen whale is known for its amazing "songs." Female humpback whales use sounds to "talk" to each other. But, only males can sing long tunes. They can sing for minutes, hours, or even days! Groups of males will sing the same songs. They even sing in tune with one another!

Some people think they sing to talk to each other or to attract females. Others believe that their songs warn other whales of danger. In 1970, some of their songs were recorded as background music to an old whaling song. It quickly became a best-selling album!

Humpbacks are also strong and playful swimmers. They slap the water with their fins and tails. Like other whales, humpbacks often launch themselves out of the water, or breach. Scientists think they might breach to get rid of small animals on their skin. Or, they might do it just for fun!

A humpback whale and calf swim to the ocean's surface.

Fin Whales

The fin whale is the second largest whale on Earth. They grow to over 80 ft. (25 m) in length and can weigh up to 160,000 lbs. (72,500 kg). That is nine times heavier than a Tyrannosaurus Rex!

Fin whales' backs and sides are black or dark gray, while their bellies are white. Their lips are dark on the left side but white on the right side. When they hunt bigger prey, they swim on their right sides. That way, the prey will not see the white. When they hunt smaller fish, they swim on their left sides. The white color stuns the fish to move into a group that is easier for the whale to eat.

Fin whales are not only known for their looks. They are also one of the fastest species of whales. They can swim about 25 mi. per hour (40 km per hour) when they are scared. Their normal pace is a steady 18 mph (30 kmph).

fin whale

74 feet (23 meters)

Female fin whales can grow up to three times as long as the biggest elephants.

LET'S EXPLORE MATH

Female fin whales are usually longer than males. In the Northern Hemisphere, adult female fin whales grow to about 74 feet long. Adult males can be about 69 feet long.

1. How much longer is the female than the male?
2. If a female and a male fin whale were swimming one right behind the other, how many feet long would they be altogether?

blue whale

The Übersee Museum in Germany has a to-scale model of a blue whale's heart.

24

Blue Whales

Blue whales are the biggest animals that have ever existed. Even the largest dinosaurs did not come close. The blue whale can grow up to 100 ft. (30 m) long and can weigh up to 400,000 lbs. (180,000 kg). And its heart can weigh as much as a small piano!

Blue whales are also the loudest animals in the world. A blue whale's heartbeat can be heard up to two miles away! And its "speech" is louder than a jet engine. Like humpback whales, blue whales "sing." Scientists think blue whales sing for many reasons. Singing helps them find their way in the dark. And it helps them find food. Their songs also let them talk to each other. Blue whales can hear each other up to 1,000 mi. (1,600 km) away. That's like yelling in London and being heard in Madrid!

Researchers photograph a blue whale in Mexico.

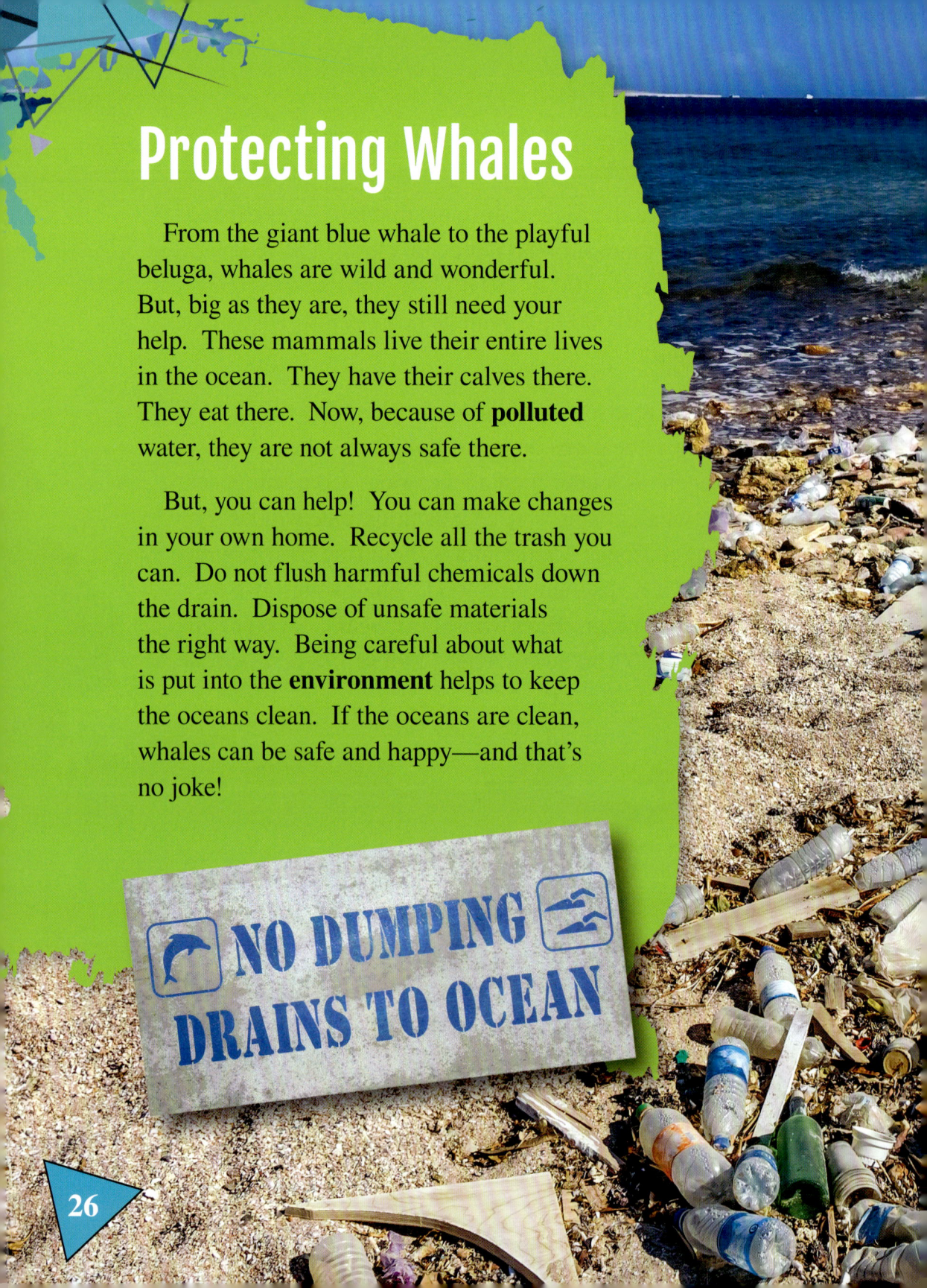

Protecting Whales

From the giant blue whale to the playful beluga, whales are wild and wonderful. But, big as they are, they still need your help. These mammals live their entire lives in the ocean. They have their calves there. They eat there. Now, because of **polluted** water, they are not always safe there.

But, you can help! You can make changes in your own home. Recycle all the trash you can. Do not flush harmful chemicals down the drain. Dispose of unsafe materials the right way. Being careful about what is put into the **environment** helps to keep the oceans clean. If the oceans are clean, whales can be safe and happy—and that's no joke!

A family separates items to be recycled.

Volunteers collect trash on the beach.

Problem Solving

A class keeps track of how many whales are spotted on a marine center's webcam in one month. They record the data in a table.

1. How many total fin whales were spotted during Week 2 and Week 3?

2. Your friend wants to know how many blue whales were spotted during the month. She adds 56, 9, 104, and 72 but realizes that her solution does not make sense. Use her work to explain the mistake. Find the correct sum.

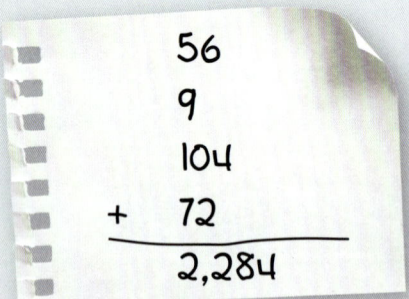

3. During week 4, 17 of the orcas spotted were calves. How many orcas were adults?

4. How many more narwhals were spotted than sperm whales during the month?

28

Whale	Week 1	Week 2	Week 3	Week 4
blue	56	9	104	72
fin	21	57	13	49
humpback	220	106	201	83
gray	152	234	132	93
sperm	30	15	47	113
orca	291	56	86	164
narwhal	73	101	10	98
beluga	47	140	168	132

Glossary

armor—a hard covering that protects something

baleen plates—two rows of hair that hang from upper jaws of baleen whales

barnacles—shellfish that attach themselves to rocks, boats, and certain whales

blowholes—holes in whales' heads used for breathing

blubber—the fat on whales and other animals that live in water

breach—to make an opening by pushing through something

denser—heavier than most things that are the same size

echolocation—the use of sound waves to determine location

environment—the natural world

mammals—animals that feed milk to their young and that usually have hair

migrations—animals moving from one place to another according to season

pods—groups of ocean animals that swim together

polluted—dirty and unsafe land, water, or air

predators—animals that survive by eating other animals

prey—animals that are hunted or killed by other animals for food

species—groups of animals or plants that are similar and can produce young animals or plants

Index

Arctic, 14, 18

baleen whale, 16, 20

beluga whale, 14–15, 26, 29

blowholes, 4, 16

blue whale, 4, 24–26, 28–29

calves, 4, 14, 18, 26, 28

fin whale, 22–23, 28–29

gray whale, 4, 17–19, 29

humpback whales, 20–21, 25, 29

mammal, 4, 18, 26

narwhals, 12–14, 28–29

orca, 4, 7–9, 28–29

pods, 8, 14

predators, 8

prey, 6, 8, 11, 13, 16, 22

species, 4, 6, 14, 20, 22

sperm whale, 10, 11, 28–29

toothed whale, 6–7, 11–12, 16

Answer Key

Let's Explore Math

page 9:
1. 90 teeth
2. 180 teeth
3. Answers will vary, but may include: Since I knew that 45 + 45 = 90, I can add 90 and 90 to find 180.

page 11:
1,150 ft.

page 13:
1. 92 narwhals
2. 45 narwhals

page 19:
1. 44 mi.
2. 28 mi.

page 23:
1. 5 ft. longer
2. 143 ft. long

Problem Solving

1. 70 fin whales
2. Answers will vary, but may include: She did not use place value to find her solution. She added tens and ones with hundreds. The correct sum is 241.
3. 147
4. 77